Marriages
ARE MADE IN
Heaven,
BUT MAINTAINED ON EARTH

Marriages are made in Heaven, but maintained on earth

JOYCELYN PEART-LAWSON

XULON PRESS

Xulon Press
2301 Lucien Way #415
Maitland, FL 32751
407.339.4217
www.xulonpress.com

© 2019 by Joycelyn Peart-Lawson

All rights reserved solely by the author. The author guarantees all contents are original and do not infringe upon the legal rights of any other person or work. No part of this book may be reproduced in any form without the permission of the author. The views expressed in this book are not necessarily those of the publisher.

Scripture quotations taken from the King James Version (KJV) – *public domain.*

GNB (also the GNT) Scripture quotations taken from the Good News Bible © 1994 published by the Bible Societies/HarperCollins Publishers Ltd UK, Good News Bible© American Bible Society 1966, 1971, 1976, 1992. Used with permission.

Printed in the United States of America.

ISBN-13: 9781545674697

Dedication

I dedicate this book to married couples, Couples engaged to be married and those who are thinking about marriage. According to the constitution of the scriptures, "whoso findeth a wife findeth a good thing, and obtaineth favor from the Lord." (Proverb 18: 22). Having entered or is thinking about entering this Holy Institution of marriage, you will find that God must be the head.

I therefore commend you for your sense of responsibility, in taking on or to have maintained your marriage, in light of the world's view that aims on eroding or breaking down the sanctity and purity of this Holy Institution.

The union as man and wife reminds our Adversary of Christ and His Bride, the Church. This makes Him mad and even the more desperate to end or contaminate relationships.

In many cases, it seemed the Devil due to his desperation to steal, kill and to destroy the joy out of marriage, has succeeded; but I have victory news for you, He cannot, unless you the husbands/wives choose to give over or yield to deception from the enemy to wreck the marriage.

With that said, you have a very important responsibility to maintain your union on earth, because it was made in heaven. And Satan, who will deviously find ways to ensure that you do not succeed in living a fun filled, memory enriched, fruitful union which by the way was originally intended from the time of creation, when the creator of all good things blessed them and said,

> *".... Be fruitful, and multiply, and replenish the earth, and subdue it: And have dominion over the fish of the sea, and over the fowl of the air, and over every living thing that moveth upon the earth." (Gen. 1:28)*

Contents

Dedication v

Preface ix

Introduction xi

Marriages Are Forever 1
   (Six) principles: 2

Treat Me Right (Sex in Marriage) 8
   Sexual Intercourse in Marriage 8
   The code of love: 12
   In my own words: 13
   Testimonial 1 15
   Life Application 16
   Her Husband so truly praises her saying: 19
   His wife so truly honors him saying: 19
   My Beloved- 20
   "Be fruitful and multiply", said the Lord: 23
   Action speaks louder than words: 24
   Become best friends, it's a wise move 25
   A True Friend (Poem) 26
   In my own words 2: 30
   No time limits on lip locks and hugs 32
   Partner together! Make decisions together! 32
   It is always healthy to have fun together as a
   couple: 33

God and Us 35

Tough love 40
    Testimonial 2............................40
    It's Hard Not To (Poem) 45

A Virtuous Woman 48
    Wives respect and obey your husbands.......48
    Testimonial 3............................50
    Wives, treat your husband's right. 51
    True beauty begins within.................54

Husband (Stand in your Priestly Position) 57
    Listen carefully 60
    Husbands do not 63

Commit to Happiness 64
    Recipe 101 (Creole Poem) 64
    Commit to: 65
    I'm committed (Poem) 66
    Express yourself:.........................70

Marriage is a Sacrifice 71
    The Love Pledge: 71
    Important to note........................74

1⇨2⇨3⇨Red Light..........................76
    Testimonial 4............................83

Conclusion 87
    Marriage is an honorable thing, commit to
    honor it.................................88

Preface

These pages are filled with tips that will come in handy on a daily basis.

The book is categorized in the following areas:

- ♥ Romantic poetry soothing to the soul.

- ♥ The infallible word of God, to bring freshness and guidance to given points made by the author.

- ♥ Insight from other couples who willingly shared their experiences during their many years of being married.

INTRODUCTION

I can clearly recall it was the day before my beautiful wedding', 25th October 2002, a dear friend of mine took me aside to encourage me. As the conversation draws to an end, she said, "Joyce, what you are entering into is not always going to be a, 'bed of rose.' There will be pot holes, and road blocks, itches and glitches. Sometimes you may even think about taking a detour out of your marriage, but do not. Because, if my husband and I could go twenty five years into marriage and still love each other, girl, I know with the help of God, you both will make it."

Seventeen years into marriage with Irving Kevin Lawson, and I have no regrets, truth be told, yes, we do have our times of differences, but I give all honor to God that we're still, 'making it', growing stronger and loving each other more. The challenges along the way only made us stronger in our relationship with God; For through it all, we have learnt to trust in Jesus and the covenant shared, "I take thee Irving Kevin Lawson, to be my lawful wedded husband, to have and to hold, from this day forward, for better, for worst, for Richer, for poorer, in sickness and in health, to love and to cherish, till death do we part, according to God's holy ordinance; and thereto I pledge thee my loyalty."

We have grown to realize that when we stood before the Alter in the presence of God, the officiating Ministers and our invited guests, we were actually at the starting line of our marriage. On your mark, get set, go! In as much as having this big hurrah and high-spirited cheers, the responsibility was ours to tread the path before us. I know that even if we walk through the valley of the shadow of death, God would be with us. Because, He endorses marriages as it was: He who at first stated that,

> "…. *it is not good that the man should be alone; I will make him an help meet for him.*" (Gen. 2:18).

Hence, the institution of marriage is considered to be Divine and as such marriage is truly made in Heaven. Like Adam and Eve, we are given the mandate to go and have dominion. Life is set before us, the facts are clear, we have Divine approval, and it is up to us to go, conquer, and maintain that which God has given.

Make it absolutely clear; we possess faith in what God has divinely instituted. But, it is up to us to do the maintenance work in the garden of life. We must endeavor to work diligently, even the more with thorns, and thistles which accompany the hard knocks life sometimes offer. But, we are encouraged that where sin abounded, God's grace did much more abound: – (Romans 5:20.)

"Marriages are Made in Heaven, but Maintained on Earth" was surely written to encourage, assist and address some practical ways that couples as well as

Introduction xiii

those who are considering this holy union, may employ to enrich their marriages and thus stay together for a lifetime.

So do you want to?

- ♥ Rekindle the fire in your marriage?

- ♥ Unleash passion in your Marriage?

- ♥ Reverse word curses spoken over the life of your marriage?

- ♥ Ensure that your husband stay in love with you, like God hath intended it to?

- ♥ Earn that respect and submission from your wife, that you so rightly deserve?

Then, I implore you, get your tools and let's go to work.

Marriages Are Forever

The feast of wheat will grind to an end. The wine may lose its savor, but the miraculous ingredient of love possessed by husbands and wives make a perfect recipe that will be on the menu for eternity.

Not to love is to lose out on the foretastes divinely originated by God for you. Love is a gift to give to all, so lavishly give it to the one closest to your heart.

<u>Love is eternal. (1Corinthians 13:8)</u>

Love is not purchased by actions or contingent upon emotions for the moment. Rather, it is a decision made on a daily basis that someone is special and valuable to you.

> *"Though I speak with the tongues of men and of angels, and have not charity, I am become as sounding brass, or a tinkling cymbal." (1 Corinthians 13:1)*

(Six) Principles:

1. Leave and Cleave: A divine connection. *"Therefore, shall a man leave his father and his mother, and shall cleave unto his wife: and they shall be one flesh. (Genesis 2:24)*

2. Marriage is a covenant made between the man, his wife, God and by extension the witnesses. God designs marriage hence, He has the solution on how to maintain, make it last. Husbands must have oneness in the relationship with their wives, bound together by the Holy Covenant.

3. Both individuals pledge to love, nurture and protect each other until death. *"Therefore what God has joined together, let no man put a sunder." (Mark 10:9)*

4. The two, now becomes one, "man and woman" by way of consummation, or commonly referred to as sexual intercourse. *"I am my beloved and my beloved is mine…." (Songs of Solomon 6:3)*

   "Two are better than one, because they have a good reward for their labor. For If they fall, the one will lift up his fellow: But woe to him that is alone when he falleth; for he hath not another to help him up. Also, if two lie down together, then they have heat: but how can one be warm alone?" (Ecclesiastes.4:9-11)

5. Be fruitful and multiply. (procreation or adoption)

6. Marriage is an holy institution set forth by God. This representation is a serious one, for its foundation is the strongest for building a family.

God is the founder of marital relationships. *Then the LORD God said, "It is not good for the man to live alone. I will make a suitable companion to help him." (Genesis 2:18)*

> *[21]Then the LORD God made the man fall into a deep sleep, and while he was sleeping, he took out one of the man's ribs and closed up the flesh. [22]He formed a woman out of the rib and brought her to him. [23]Then the man said, "At last, here is one of my own kind—- Bone taken from my bone, and flesh from my flesh.'Woman' is her name because she was taken out of man."*

> *[24]That is why a man leaves his father and mother and is united with his wife, and they become one. (Genesis 2: 22-24)*

7. Marriage came about so that man can have a companion. *"But from the beginning of creation, God made them male and female. For this cause shall a man leave his father and mother and cleave to his wife; and the two will become one flesh. So they twain shall be one flesh: So then they are no more twain, but one flesh. What therefore, God hath joined together, let no man put asunder."(Mark 10:6-9)*

8. God gave marriage as a gift to Adam and Eve. *"May your fountain be blessed, and may you rejoice in the wife of your youth. A loving doe, a graceful deer-"May may her breasts satisfy you always, may you ever be intoxicated with her love." (Proverbs. 5:18-19)*

9. Marriage is sacred, respect its sacrosanct. *"For your Maker is your husband, the LORD of hosts is His name; and the Holy One of Israel is your Redeemer, the God of the whole earth he is called."* **(Isaiah 54:5)**

10. Marriage brings joy and fulfillment, to a soul plagued with loneliness.

11. Yes, marriages can hold times of temporary sadness if you know what to do. Rebuke the spirit of sadness and invite the Spirit of joy and gladness.

12. Married couples salute patience and longsuffering. *"Love is patient, love is kind. It is not proud. It does not dishonor others, it is not self-seeking, it is not easily angered, and it keeps no records of wrongs." (1 Corinthians 13:4-5)*

13. Marriage provides deeper companionship and fellowship. *"Let the morning bring me word of your unfailing love, for I have put my trust in you. Show me the way I should go, for to you I entrust my life. (Psalm. 143:8)*

14. Marriage bears the weight of trust and obedience. Wives submit and obey your husbands. And husbands love and trust your wives. *"Let marriage be*

> *held in honor among all, and let the marriage bed be undefiled, for God will judge the sexually immoral and adulterous." (Hebrew.13:4)*

15. Marriage is grounded upon a godly and stable commitment by the couple. *"And over all these virtues put on love, which binds them all together in perfect unity." (Colossians 3:14)*

16. Marriage calls forth passion and compassion for and of each spouse. Do not communicate with each other for a week and see what happens. The withdrawal syndrome will step in.

17. Marriage is based on love in action and not feelings only. Speak it with your mouth and act it out with your body.

18. Marriage is honorable, commit to honor.

19. Marriage is blessed by God, commit to blessing God. *In the good times, praise His name. In the bad times, do the same. In everything, give the King of Kings all the praise. (lyrics by Donna Alley)*

20. Marriage is until death, commit to your marriage until death.

> *...to avoid fornication, let every man have his own wife, and let every woman have her own husband. Let the husband render unto the wife true benevolence: And like wise the wife unto the*

> *husband. The wife hath not power of her own body, but the husband: and likewise the husband hath not power of his own body, but the wife. Defraud ye not one the other expect it be with consent for a time, that ye may give your selves to fasting and prayer: and come together again, that Satan tempts you not for your incontinency–(1 Corinthians 7: 1-5)*

You are my Eros[a] love; I yearn to be united with you. The desire to possess the romantic, passionate and sentimental experiences shared during consummation.

You are my Storage[b], the natural affection and sense of belonging derived from being around you.

You are my Philio[c]; the new ventures shared, endless hours talking and reflecting, interesting rewards gained through communicating.

You are my Agape[d]; the culmination of our romance is unselfish and has the capacity to keep giving to you my love. It's the strong binding force that propels us closer to each other guaranteeing the lasting success of our marriage with God has our Head.

My heart, you are my vibrating sensual master of love.

21. Marriage is the perfect solution for loneliness. *It's not good for man to be alone. (Genesis 2:18)*

22. Marriage is ordained by God for two persons who are desirous of spending a lifetime being each other's lifeline.

23. Marriage should only be terminated by death not separation or divorce – the ideal.

24. Marriage symbolizes the union that exists between Christ and His bride the Church. Christ gave his life for is bride, in order for her to have eternal life.

25. Marriage is not to be taken lightly; neither should it be entered into immaturely. Counseling is important before taking this breath-taking step.

26. Marriage creates the best atmosphere for raising children. *"Children obey your parents in the lord for this is right." (Ephesians 6:1) "Children, obey your parents in all things: for this is well pleasing unto the Lord." (Colossians 3:20)*

Treat Me Right
(Sex in Marriage)

Sexual Intercourse in Marriage

God did not design sex for infatuation or selfish gratification, but for the pleasure of a man and his wife. It is the satisfaction that climaxes their intimate relation.

27. Sex in marriage is great, for God created it to be so. You enter the sexual court sad, depress and stress. I can testify to you, you will never leave the same way you came in Jesus name.

28. First sex is sweeter, second sex last longer. *e.g. Make love at 7:00, last about fifteen minutes but it was sweet. However, half an hour, maybe an hour later you take the same ride it did not only taste better but last longer; yum, yum.*

29. Bed sex is great. But what about the other furniture? Do not be afraid to explore.

30. Show great interest in intimacy with your spouse. Tell him or her where you get pleasure the most. How will he know if you don't tell or show?

31. Change locations when making love.

32. Hard surface, deeper penetration. Especially for husbands with a smaller size penis.

33. Sex in marriage is voluntary; it is a gift to celebrate.

34. Sex is pleasurable when you express it in the act of love making. You can't just lie down and say, 'take it, take it', and expect your spouse to enjoy it. That type of mentality is of the devil. Rebuke it in Jesus name. *"Do everything in love." (1 Corinthians. 16:14)*

35. While making love, share love talk, it raises the sexual stakes.

36. Try as often as possible to reach climax together. Let her have the pleasure of coming 1, 2, and 3, times and she will give you the medals. It's a win, win situation. Your manhood, and her stress relief medication.

37. A sexual union creates a soul-tie, you are bond together spiritually.

38. Sometimes your spouse may ask for an early morning or a late night "quickie", don't leave

them hanging because it's not your thing. May I remind you that your body does not belong to you but to your spouse; *"The wife hath not owner of her own body, but the husband: and likewise also the husband hath not power of his own body, but the wife." (1 Corinthians 7:4)*

39. After love-making, you can talk to your partner about anything. Chances are he/she will be too satisfied and tired to debate it. It may or may not work for you but you can give it a try.

40. Sex is more than flesh to flesh for erotic pleasure; instead it is a spiritual bonding of the soul. The act clears the mind; confusion is a thing of the past when you yield yourself to sexual pleasure, trust me it's true.

41. Sex helps the husband to learn more about his wife. What excites her, and her dislikes.

42. Sex reveals to the wife the rhythm of her soul-mate. 'A little to the right please. Yes, that's right. Ahhhh'

43. Sexual excitement unveils sweet lyrical messages, to the one closes to you. 'Oh baby, you make my world spin. Your rides are sweeter than Coney Park or Disney land.'

44. Sex causes one to multiply, and replenish the earth. I reserve any comment/s on birth control. It is up to each couple to decide.

45. A healthy sex life is very important to a man and a woman, for it keeps them healthy and strong.

46. It is quite natural to make love more than once for the same night.

47. If only one partner reaches climax during love-making, don't wait two, three days before you try to make it up with your unfulfilled partner.

48. Pray and ask God to help you to satisfy your spouse. Set the right atmosphere, make the right moves and take your spouse to the haven of orgasm.

49. Making love in the light, dispel the idea that your spouse does not want to see you in all your glory. It also helps you to discover a unique mark on your spouse's body, talk about it.

50. Timely watch body movements, keenly listen to rhythmic breathing, then you'll know when to welcome enjoyment, climax and fulfillment.

51. Massage your spouse's upper and lower body parts (breasts/penis); create stiffness and elongation. There to welcoming excitement and fulfillment.

52. Create excitement in love- making.

    ♥ Try different positions and enjoy the intensity of the moment. Be creative like, sharing how much you enjoy love-making.

♥ Try the waters; see how deep it is so that you'll know how far to venture.

53. Bring newness to your sex life; explore, navigate and investigate, the findings will be to your liking.

The Code of Love:

54. Carefully approach.

55. Purposefully enter.

56. Creatively and precisely react.

57. Confidently climax.

58. Sincerely talk.

59. Quietly go off to sleep

60. Satisfactorily rejuvenated.

61. Believe it or not, sex **HELPS!** *"Let the morning bring me word of your unfailing love, for I have put my trust in you. Show me the way I should go, for to you I entrust my life."*

Heavy Breathing: Sex raises your oxygen in cells helping organs and tissues to function at their peaks.

Exercise: Sex is exercise; it can reduce your risk of major illnesses, such as heart disease, stroke, diabetes and cancer by up to 50% and lower your risk of early death by up to 30%.[1]

Lower Cholesterol: Regular love making breaks down fatty tissues in the body.

Pain Relief: Sex can lower arthritic pain and headache.

Stress Relief: Sex is a very good antidote to reduce stress.

Leave your total dependence and your allegiance to your parents. Cleave only and solely to your spouse. "Become one". *"The flowers have already appeared in the land; the time has arrived for pruning the vines, and the voice of the turtledove has been heard in our land. The fig tree has ripened its figs, and the vines in blossom have given forth their fragrance. Arise, my darling, my beautiful one, and come along!'" – (Song of Solomon 2:12)*

62. Serious meditation on how to enrich your marriage.
    "There is no fear in love, but perfect love drives out fear, because fear involves punishment. The one who fears has not been perfected in love." (1 John 4:18)

63. Work with your spouse; allow him/her to strive to be the best. Encourage continuous education to unfulfilled dreams. This will help the self-esteem.

❡IN MY OWN WORDS:

Eat the spiritual fruit and open you sexual appetite.

64. Feast on the fruit of the Spirit. *"For to set the mind on the flesh is death, but to set the mind on the Spirit is life and peace." {Romans 8:6}*

65. Eat Humility *"Humble yourself before the Lord, and he will lift you up." {James 4:10}*

66. Grow love and in love. *"Love must be sincere. Hate what is evil; cling to what is good. Be devoted to one another in love. Honor one another above yourselves." (Romans 12:9-10)*

67. Breathe the fresh air of joy. *"Rejoice always, pray continually, and give thanks in all circumstances; for this is God's will for you in Christ Jesus." (1 Thessalonians 5:16-18)*

68. Eat and regurgitate patience. *"May the God who gives endurance and encouragement give you the same attitude of mind toward each other that Christ Jesus had."(Romans 15:5)*

69. Trod on the path of peace. *"Blessed are the peacemakers, for they shall be called sons of God. (Matthew.5:9)*

70. Mingle a while with longsuffering.

71. Practice the action word faith.

72. Exercise temperance, it's a life line in a life time.

73. Speak life into your marriage relationship.

74. Be willing to make sacrifices that will improve your relationship with your spouse.

75. Make restitution, after a lovers' quarrel. *"Peace I leave with you; my peace I give to you. Not as the world gives do I give to you. Let not your hearts be troubled, neither let them be afraid."* (St. John 14:27)

76. Sustain the marriage with the remedy known as communication. *"Make haste, my beloved, and be thou like a roe or to a young hart upon the mountains of spices."* (Solomon 8: 14)

TESTIMONIAL 1

A young couple married for only (4) four years, started exchanging unkind words to each other. The tsunami of unkind words thrown across the husband and wife's marital bed heightened the wife's frustration; she lashed at her husband demanding he bring her back to her mother's house. It was told to me that the husband threw the fan given to them for a wedding present, hitting the bed room door.

The bride broke down in an ocean of tears, when she saw her love crying on the bed-room floor; Overwhelmed by seeing the tears streaming down his cheeks, she totally forgot about the fact that she wanted to leave the relationship. Her love for him was stronger than the string of unkind words. She wanted more to console him and tell him she was sorry for causing him hurt.

There, broken by their first lovers' quarrel, they promised each other that if or when there was arising conflict again, they would refrain from speaking unkind words from their lips to each other. They hugged, apologized to each other and finally, prayed and broke the curses released over each other's life out of anger.

After the wife recounted the story, with a broad smile on her face, she told the group that her honey moon night had no comparison to the passion shared that faithful night. I dubbed it, "The Lovers' Quarrel."

¶Life Application

77. Pay attention to your spouse's spoken and especially unspoken words. *"Wherefore, my beloved brethren, let every man be swift to hear, slow to speak, slow to wrath." (James. 1:19)*

78. Kiss your spouse each night before going to bed. Let it be your spiritual prescribed medication for remembered love. *"Every good gift and every perfect gift is from above, and cometh down from the Father of lights, with whom is no variableness, neither shadow of turning."(James. 1:17)*

79. Give your spouse a second bath with your tongue, instead of using it to tear him or her down. By doing this, it helps to relax the mind and soothe the emotion. Believe me, I've experienced it. *In other words, use your tongue to link your spouse's body. Don't use it to speak unkind words to him or her.*

80. Wet kisses on your spouse's body will heal the sores of loneliness. *"Complete my joy by being of the*

same mind, having the same love, being in full accord and of one mind." (Philippians 2:2)

81. Know when to give marital space or just alone time with God. *"Do not deprive each other of sexual relations, unless you both agree to refrain from sexual intimacy for a limited time, so you can give yourself more completely to prayer. Afterward you shall come together again so that Satan won't be able to tempt you because of your lack of self control."(1 Corinthians 7:5)*

82. Experiment on your spouse to find where his/her sweet spots are, 'sexual hotspots'. *Touch different parts of your spouse's body, to know where brings excitement and sexual arousals.*

83. Feel and send the light pole into the gold mine of love and wetness. *Husbands, gently massage your wife's clitoris, (the pleasure center of the vulva) this is found above the vaginal opening and the urethra. Then with great assurance, insert your manhood into her lubricated vagina.*

The Clitoris is the primary source of the female sexual pleasure; direct stimulation is usually needed for the final push into climax.

84. Feel your way across his/her "dark hair forest" of love. *Move your fingers across the pubic hair of your spouse if there is any. Some couples may choose to shave. But if there is any there, do it, it should be fun.*

85. Explore the lawful seas of passion, (vagina). Take a speed boat or a long canoe (penis). Make passionate love!

86. Relax in your garden of love, stay awhile. Catch a breath, after all that heavy breathing. *After love making, don't just jump off the bed and into the shower, or turning your back on your spouse to sleep. Instead, lie in each other's arms, and reflect on the passion just shared.*

87. Husbands, venture the area of enchantment. There are no creatures, only lubrication that awaits another round of ejaculation. *Take that beautiful venture into making love; don't be afraid you may not fulfill your partner. When you get there, the only thing that awaits you is lubrication from the vagina, welcoming the sexual master of love. Be bold; be strong, for the Lord your God is with you.*

88. Taste and feel, be mesmerize by his/her sight, feel the aroma.

> [22]*Wives, submit yourselves unto your own husbands, as unto the Lord.* [23]*For the husband is the head of the wife, even as Christ is the head of the church: and he is the savor of the body.* [24]*Therefore as the church is subjected unto Christ, so let the wives; be to their own husbands in everything.*
>
> [25]*Husbands love your wives, even as Christ so love the church and gave*

> *himself for it; ²⁶That he might sanctify and cleanse it with the washing of water by the word, ²⁷That he might present it to himself a glorious church, not having spot or wrinkle, or any such thing; but that it should be holy and without blemish. ²⁸So ought men to love their wives as their own bodies. He that loveth his wife loveth himself.*
> *(Ephesians. 5: 21-28)*

Her Husband so truly praises her saying:

Many are those who have done nobly, but you my love excel them all. You are my glory, my greatest achievement, unique and sweet. You are a living demonstration of the qualities I possess. You my love are my neck and I am the head. There is no one closer to uphold and encourage me. My beloved, when my eyes gazed at your radiance, it shines and reflects me your soul-mate. I delight myself in you my wife.

His wife so truly honors him saying:

My friend, my lover, my husband and lord, thou art the sun and I am the moon; for the moon is the glory of the sun. My only beauty comes when you glow my precious. You provide, love and protect, I feel secure for you are my security. I love you from now and unto eternity. My love, your love for God reflects in your love for me and your family.

My Beloved-

89. I am my beloved and my beloved is mine.

90. My beloved, thou art wonderfully made and made to be wonderful.

91. My beloved, the weapons of our warfare are not carnal. And the carnal weapons are not ours.

92. My beloved, as you are hidden in Christ Jesus, So am I in your ever-growing love.

93. My beloved, you are the spring within my dessert places.

94. My beloved, you are my garden of nuts that I would go nuts for.

95. My beloved, you are my main course I order every night.

96. My beloved, the roof of your mouth is as unto a gig-saw puzzle, a game I love to play.

97. My beloved, your saliva mixed with mine results in the creation of us making the finest saliva wine.

98. My beloved, you allow my closed and shy lips to part as Moses parting the red sea. I will endeavor drowning in your love.

99. My beloved, you are the lilies among my thrones, glow and grow and suffocate those unwanted weeds that wants to take your place.

100. My beloved, I will shower you with my kisses, dry you with tender loving care and clothe you with my love. You will never feel empty or naked.

Spouse; do not be afraid to express yourself using sound words intertwined with sweetness. And when you have run out of words, feel free to borrow a few lines from King Solomon. *"Let him kiss me with the kisses of his mouth: for thy love is better than wine." {Songs of Solomon. 1:1}*

> *"Love sufferth long, and is kind, is not puffed up, doeth not behave itself unseemly, seeketh not its own, is not provoked, taketh not account for evil, rejoiceth not in uun- righteousness, but rejoiceth with the truth."*
> *(1 Corinthians. 13:4-6)*

Allow your spouse to be wowed! Make the time, and:

- ♥ Clip nails
- ♥ Scrub the sole of feet
- ♥ Shave each other
- ♥ Brush hair
- ♥ Massage back
- ♥ Tweeze hair from face
- ♥ Bath your spouse; give the back a good scrub.

101. Remind each other that the marriage is permanent and not temporary.

102. Laugh, pray and cry together as a couple.

103. As often as possible reach climax together.

104. Stir up the erotic gift that's in side every Lover. *"The flowers have already appeared in the land; the time has arrived for pruning the vines, and the voice of the turtledove has been heard in our land. The fig tree has ripened its figs, and the vines in blossom have given forth their fragrance. Arise, my darling, my beautiful one, and come along!"* – *(Solomon 2:12-13)*

105. Motivate each other in love making.

106. Saturate your emotional atmosphere with the words of God.

107. Electrify the mind of your spouse with spirit-filled thoughts.

108. Modify your love making techniques. Do not be stagnant in love making techniques. It will only get better. Orgasm is the height in which you must attain.

"BE FRUITFUL AND MULTIPLY", SAID THE LORD:

109. Marriage is to procreate children. If the marriage does not bear fruit, extend your love by adopting.

110. Provide, protect and produce.

111. Show kindness to your spouse and family.

112. On special occasions, take pictures of your spouse and family.

113. Read stories to your children and enjoy rapping with them.

114. Plan at least one family vacation for the year.

115. Familiarize yourself with the music your children listen to.

116. Do not give your children the impression that you are too busy for them.

117. Give love and endless support to your spouse and family.

118. Have at least one activity you do together as a family.

119. Do not be a child abuser but rather role model in the home.

120. Spend quality time with your nuclear family.

121. As often as you can, hug and tell your child/ children that you love him/her or them.

ACTION SPEAKS LOUDER THAN WORDS:

122. Accept your spouse's strengths and patiently work on weaknesses.

123. Stand by your heart beat in the good times and the bad.

124. Stand complete in the splendor of your unending love.

125. Work together has a couple, build stripes of love, compassion and togetherness.

126. Couples should endeavor to put each other in prayer always. In each other's presence and out.

127. Couples should feast on materials that will help in the nourishment and survival of the marital relationship. One such book is the Holy Book. 'Bible'

128. Comfort in sickness, support in pain, love through conflict, stick it through to the end.

129. Trust in the Lord and lean not to your own understanding, in all your ways acknowledge God, and He will direct your path.

130. Pay quality attention to your listening skills, and watch attentively with your eyes.

131. Encourage dialogue not monologue; it's one of the lifelines in the marriage.

132. Mutual agreement on decision making. Disagreements will spring up, but this weed killer call compromise, will kill it at the roots.

133. Plan spontaneous events to satisfy the eagerness of reaching home. This will hasten your spouse's steps in returning home.

134. Learn to communicate with your spouse- break down the walls of overnight conflicts within 24 hours.

135. The ideal; only death should give way to a second marriage.

Cremate the thought of unfaithfulness; scatter the ash to the wind of the Spirit who will blow it as far as the east is from the west in your marriage.

Become best friends, it's a wise move.

A TRUE FRIEND (POEM)

A friend is kind, honest and true.

A friend is loyal and does not play a righteous fool.

A friend will share in the joy and sorrow.

A friend is one you can lean on and not be afraid that you will fall.

A friend will give you good advice, and never lead you astray.

Whatever you do, whatever you say that friend will never walk away.

(Joycelyn Lawson)

"For this cause shall a man leave father and mother, and shall cleave to his wife: and they twain shall be one flesh. ⁶Wherefore they are no more twain but one flesh. What therefore God hath put together let not man put a sunder. (Matthew. 19:5-6)

136. Cut the navel string of allegiance to parents or anyone who may become a treat to causing conflict in your marital union.

137. Turn your love antenna only on your spouse. *"Let love and faithfulness never leave you; bind them around your neck, write them on the tablet of your heart. Then you will win favor and a good name in the sight of God and man." (Proverbs. 3:3-4)*

138. Wow your spouse with poetic lines flooding with passionate thoughts from the heart. 'Send your lips my way, so has to decorate them with mine.'

139. Make beautiful harmony while dubbing, flesh of my flesh and bone of bone.

140. Pay expensive attention to your soul-mate, allowing him or her to feel the weight of your presence, and the softness of your warm embrace.

141. Play seducing games with your spouse; bring the sexual stakes higher. The more rounds you win are the more clothes that come off. This is real fun! The one who loses still wins for pleasure is the trophy given to both players.

142. Flirtation is the name of this 'balls' game, played by only two who are deeply in love and who are not ashamed to express it by romancing in the rain.

143. Regularly remind your spouse why you got married in the first place, refresh the memories and recreate them all over again. The bad ones learn from them and pledge you will try not to let it happen again.

144. Be locked away for life, in the prison of love with your security guard who feeds you only with love.

145. Stay married it is an honorable decision: *"Marriage is honorable in all, and the bed is undefiled: Whoremongers and adulterers God will judge. (Hebrew 13:4)*

146. Don't ever give your BUN!

147. Cheating weakens the foundation of a solid marriage. And eventually, the wall which is the fencing of God will come crashing down.

148. Don't sleep around to keep your sexual appetite afloat. The pleasure is sure but the guilt is lasting.

149. Eliminate anything that will cause you to lose out on the foretastes of creating new memories with your spouse.

150. Focus not only on the physical but also on the spiritual, for if your spouse is connected to the great creator, then the marriage will bear fruit of joyful cheers and less on quarrels and unfruitful gestures.

151. Do not linger in unreal expectations. Your spouse will flourish when he/she knows you are supportive.

152. Be truthful to your spouse, and let not the sun go down on your wrath.

153. Break the strong-hold of unfulfillment in the act of love making. The number one priority is to ensure pleasure in the relationship.

154. Crush the head of pride; it normally arises when confrontations occurs and or quarrels blossoms.

155. Break the back of boredom within the marriage by becoming flexible in your sexual styles, and creative in your social ethnicity.

156. Electrocute the thought of divorce. Don't invite it in your conversations. If it knocks at your matrimonial door do not entertain it. Dismiss it and send it back from whence it came, 'The pit of hell.'

157. Shone contentment in another man's/woman's arms, for if you get too comfortable you are silently saying that the arms of your lawful spouse is not warm enough. That is not of God; if he/she has a problem causing spiritual separation, consult the head of the relationship. He can make right, what went wrong.

158. Relinquish the thoughts of disrespecting or dishonoring your spouse. *"Receive him therefore in the Lord with all gladness; and hold such reputation."{Philippians. 2:29}*

159. Put a siege on bad influence in your life, whether by friends or family. They will feed you unhealthy habits and breed the spirit of failure in your marriage.

160. Self-centeredness tears down relation that was once strengthened by dialog; selflessness strengthens the wall of love in the union. *"Nevertheless, to avoid fornication; let every man have his own wife and let every woman have her own husband." (1 Corinthians. 7:2)*

IN MY OWN WORDS 2:

161. Disregard Hatred! *"Better is a dinner of herbs where love is, than a stalled ox and hatred therewith." {Proverbs. 15:17}*

162. Divorce Adultery. *"Thou shalt not commit adultery." {Exodus.20:14}*

163. Flee ever far from witchcraft and word curse. *"And I will cut off witchcrafts out of thine hand; and thou shalt have no more soothsayers." {Micah 5:12}*

164. Part ways with emulation. *"If by any means I may provoke emulation them which are in the flesh, and might save some of them." {Romans.11:14}*

165. Dispel Sedition. Sedition means Division- *"Now I beseech you, brethren, mark them which cause divisions and offences contrary to the doctrine which ye have learned; and avoid them." {Romans. 16:17}*

166. Bound Strife. *"For where envying and strife is, there is confusion and every evil work." {James 3:16}*

167. Band Wrath. *"A fool's wrath is presently known: but a prudent man covereth shame." {Proverbs. 12:16}*

Treat Me Right (Sex in Marriage) 31

168. Crucify Lasciviousness- means thoughts being driven by sex. *"Remove thy way far from her, and come not nigh the door of her house:" {Proverbs. 5:8}*

169. Avoid communication break-down.

170. Shone the very thought of lying in a bed of thrones because your flesh is itching for the taste of adultery. Those feeling that entices you must die a horrible death in your mind. Please have the mind of Christ.

171. Instead, look attractive, handsome, and or sexy for your spouse and turn back his desire to you. That move is the right one to make.

172. Learn/study the physical gestures locomotion must be wise and prey upon them to please your spouse.

173. Harmful words should not be a part of your marital vocabulary. Think before speaking in anger, the lighter your words are, the easier it will be to swallow if taking them back.

174. Sometimes you will need to meet your spouse half way, instead of wondering who will make that first move.

175. Be excited when seeing your spouse.

176. Be ecstatic when touching your spouse.

177. Be attentive when hearing sweet honey-coated words spoken by your spouse.

178. Be hungry, yearn the knowledge imparted from the heart of your spouse to you. You complement each other; he will not lead you astray from the marital way.

179. Allow tongue and tongue to greet on a regular basis. They are twins don't keep them apart for too long.

180. Tongue bath and love bites are appreciated too.

No time limits on lip locks and hugs.

Partner together! Make decisions together!

181. Put in place an insurance plan for security purposes.

182. Break free from, you have your account, and I have mine.

183. Have an open relationship, where you both can share and discuss arising matters in the marital relationship.

184. Share future goals, aspiration, lost dreams if there are any and the vision where you see yourself in years to come. That will help your spouse to position him/her self, and dismiss unexpected surprises. *"And let us consider how we may spur one another on toward love and good deeds, not giving up*

meeting together, as some are in the habit of doing, but encouraging one another—and all the more as you see the Day approaching." (Hebrews 10:24-25)

185. Discuss the tools needed to reach those goals and budget accordingly.

186. Celebrate the conclusion, with dinner and a movie, or a trip to a resort, or oasis. *"Be devoted to one another in love. Honor one another above yourselves." (Romans 12:10)*

¶It is always healthy to have fun together as a couple:

187. Eat together around the table as a family, do it as often as possible.

188. Engage in fruitful discussions and dine away.

189. Communicate about each other's day, and then comment appropriately. This technique draws you closer, which leaves no space for the devil.

190. Play scrabble, it triggers you mentally, and if you wins you can have your spouse sexually.

191. Shower together; get the hard to reach spots that frequently only gets water.

192. Give hot oil massages, which will relief the tension built up over the days, weeks, months and years.

193. Practice having family devotions, if not once, twice a week. As your relationship grows your love for the Lord grows too.

God and Us

Likewise ye younger, submit yourselves unto the elder. Yea, all of you be subjected one to the other, and be clothed with humility: for God resisteth the proud, and giveth grace to the humble. ⁶Humble yourselves therefore to the mighty hand of God, that ye may exalt you in due time: ⁷Casting all your cares upon him; for he careth for you. ⁸Be sober; be vigilant; because your adversary the devil, as a roaring lion, walketh about seeking whom he may devour. (1 Peter 5: 5-8)

194. Learn how to love God and God will teach you how to love your spouse. *"And so we know and rely on the love God has for us. God is love. Whoever lives in love lives in God and God in them.." (1 John 4:16)*

195. Speak passionately about God, and the passion will be fueled by God towards your spouse.

196. Spend quality time locked away with God, and he will prepare you mentally when locked away with your spouse.

197. Share intimately with God, and He will unleash the power of love when sharing intimately with your spouse.

198. Endeavor to praising God minutely, hourly, daily and you will find the glory in praising and adoring your spouse minutely, hourly and daily.

199. Have Godly fear, and you will attract the fear of God upon your marriage.

200. Be a servant leader for God, and he will favor you with a servitudes heart towards your spouse.

201. Embrace each other with the fact that it is no more me/you, but US.

202. Expect good fruits once your roots are grounded deep in Jesus Christ.

203. Expect explosion of internal blessings, if you bless God in season and out of season.

204. Expect a good harvest in the future, if you have planted good seeds in the fertile soil who is Christ Jesus.

205. Expect empowerment from God to manage the affairs of your home, if you seek him earnestly for empowerment. Live and serve Him righteously.

206. Show yourself approve unto God, serve Him in humility and love, and you will receive the benefits of a long healthy marriage. *"And so we know and rely*

God and Us 37

on the love God has for us. God is love. Whoever lives in love lives in God, and God in them." (1 John 4:16)

207. Pursue Holiness as a couple, and holiness will reign in your relationship. There will be no room for extra-marital affair. *"Be ye holy, for I am holy." (1 Pet. 1:16)*

208. Submit to the head of all matrimonial bliss, and submission will come naturally in the union.

209. God is not the author of confusion; hence, understanding, confusion will weaken and die in the marriage. *"Be completely humble and gentle; be patient, bearing with one another in love." (Ephesians. 4:2)*

210. Visit the holy of Holies together as a couple, and God will speak to you both as a couple.

211. God will war against your enemies, if you stay on his side.

> *"Therefore, gird your minds for action, keep sober in spirit, fix your hope completely on the grace to be brought to you at the revelation of Jesus Christ. As obedient children do not be conformed to the former lusts which were yours in your ignorance, but like the holy one who called you." (1 Pet. 13:15)*

212. Worshipping together, welcomes the Spirit of God to rest in the marital relationship.

213. Speak truth, and truth will prevail in your union.

214. Saturate the atmosphere with praise, and the devil won't stand a chance in your marriage.

215. March around your Jericho problems in your spirit 'together', and they will crumble in the midst of your praise and worship 'together'.

216. Have in your corner a Samuel or an Elizabeth.

217. Make Christ the foundation of your marriage and it will never sink or collapse.

218. Trust God and not Viagra to make your marriage last.

219. Live under the blood of Jesus, present your marriage daily before God's throne.

220. Pursue peace in your relationship, and the God of peace will pursue you. *"Peace I leave with you; my peace I give to you. Not as the world gives do I give to you. Let not your hearts be troubled, neither let them be afraid." (St. John. 14:27)*

221. Establish the name of Jesus in your life and the life of your spouse.

222. Make straight the road you trod, and Christ will straighten the crooked path in your marriage.

223. Study the bible together, let the words of God germinate in your life's as a couple.

224. Fast and pray together, the answer will come quicker.

225. Pray that God will maximize each other potential.

226. Acquire emotional, spiritual and physical healing from God.

227. Pray for your spouse; cover her/his back from the snares of the enemy.

228. Anoint your spouse's feet with blessed olive oil.

229. Speak words of life in his/her life as well as the marriage union. 'But you my love are a chosen generation, a royal priesthood, a holy nation, a peculiar people; you my heart, will continue to show forth the praises of Him who hath called you out of darkness and into His marvelous light.

230. God is the up lifter of your head husbands, and your wives are the helper of your strength. Learn the ways of the Lord, walk in His pre-steps and be ordered by His words.

Tough Love

Testimonial 2

I knew that my husband and I were destined to be together and to create havoc in the kingdom of darkness. Terrorize the devil and his cohorts. Helping married couples to: rekindle their fire, enrich their love for each other.

It was two months before we covenanted in marriage that the enemy tried to terminate our lives. As we journeyed to a funeral service in Westmoreland, located on the south side of the island of Jamaica, the vehicle in which we were driving got out of control. Visualize-: the hill on the right, the sea on the left, and the narrow stretch of road before us.

The vehicle swerved about three times, I remembered crying out Oh God, Oh God, while holding on to the steering wheel from the passenger seat. Yes, my Finance was the driver, and I too tried to help at that terrifying moment.

You ask, so what was your husband to be reaction? Well, he was amazingly cautious and calm, not a sweat on the outside, but deep down I knew he was scared. All I know is that he held on to the steering wheel.

I saw two other hands balancing the vehicle into a straight position. I don't know how the vehicle stopped, but with great conviction I knew it was God. God intervened in our midst and set straight what the devil curved and swerved, God took control of that vehicle that day.

After the vehicle stopped and we reflected on, "what should have been, but did not happen", a smile saturated my face when the love of my life told me that he too saw the hands of God; immediately, I started crying again. We gave thanks, and praised God for his deliverance and cautiously continued unto our final destination.

I wasn't driving that faithful day, but I saw every pot holes, the meter gauge was below 70 seventy, and I tried not to perturb my spirit about our horrifying experience, but rather reflect on how God came through for my soul-mate and I.

The point is, when God sets out to do something in you and through you the enemy will try to distract and attack you, so that you will never fulfill your mandate, goal or objective.

Like that scary experience we had, so it will be at times in your life the enemy will try to crash your marriage, it will become freighting but trust God to take the wheels and to stare you through those horrific moments.

231. Weigh your likes and dislikes, then try and work around them while adjusting them.

232. Take the initiative to be a better spouse. Don't allow your spouse to feel like a door mat. *"Nevertheless, let every one of you in particular so love his wife as himself and the wife see that she reverence her husband." (Ephesians. 5:33)*

233. Do not withhold your body from your spouse. Whether you are angry or not, if he/she asks you to come into him/her, with joy take that journey, you won't ever regret it. *"The wife does not have authority over her own body but yields it to her husband. In the same way, the husband does not have authority over his own body but yields to his wife." (1 Corinthians 7:4)*

234. Privately speak of past relationships if any, and enforce the fact that your spouse was the best choice.

235. Monitor the tone in which you speak to your spouse, especially when in the company of others. *"Soft answer turneth away wrath, but grievous words stir up anger." (Proverbs 15:1)*

236. Express yourself so that your spouse can easily understand you. *"With all humility and gentleness, with patience, bearing with one another in love, eager to maintain the unity of the spirit in the bond of peace." (Ephesians. 4:2-3)*

237. Ensure that you and your spouse dress down the words spoken to each other in the time of conflicts, remember, *"A soft answer turneth away wrath: but grievous words stir up anger."(Proverbs. 15:1*

238. Blow steam, but do not burn your spouse. Be angry but sin not. Remember angry rest in the bosom of fools. *"Be not hasty in thy spirit to be angry: for anger resteth in the bosom of fools." (Ecclesiastes. 7:9)*

239. Tell your spouse when something is wrong with you. *"And over all these virtues put on love, which binds them all together in perfect unity." (Colossians. 3:14)*

240. Tell your spouse to try and bear with you in your low seasons, for they will come.

241. If you feel inadequate and unsure of yourself, share it with your spouse.

242. Breathe integrity into your marriage.

243. Find tangible ways of renewing your passion. *"Above all, love each other deeply, because love covers over a multitude of sins." (1 Peter. 4:8)*

244. Be able to adopt and tolerate.

245. Get to know your spouse on another level.

246. Start your mornings with prayer; it's a good spiritual breakfast.

247. Ten seconds of wet kissing every morning will keep you moist during parched days.

248. Focus on the relationship, let it be first priority.

249. Acknowledge your duties as a spouse.

250. Pursue happiness in the relationship, its good medicine.

251. Let your friendship as a couple grow and mature.

252. Send birthday cards and personal notes to your spouse on those special days.

253. Find out what your spouse is thinking on a regular basis.

254. Speak peace within the marriage. *"Be kind to each other, tenderhearted, forgiving one another, just as God through Christ has forgiven you."(Ephesians 4:32)*

255. Periodically see where more time is spent.

256. Avoid making promises to your spouse that you just can't fulfill.

257. Pool in your resources as a couple, share costs

258. Try and build a good relationship with the parents or guardians of your spouse.

259. Develop realistic goals and expectations.

260. Smiles and laughing are good remedies to keep in the love chest of your relationship.

261. Utilize technology to transmit signals of love to your spouse; this will surely make his/her day.

262. Encourage your spouse not to be like someone else, but rather be him/her self.

263. When you share with your spouse, share from your heart.

264. Show concern by asking questions such as:
    - ♥ How was your day today?
    - ♥ Are you okay?
    - ♥ Are you enjoying my company?
    - ♥ How can I please you more?
    - ♥ How was my love making this week?

It's Hard Not To (Poem)

Joycelyn Lawson

It's hard not to be around you, it's dead hard not to be close to you. It is so hard not to be with you; when my love deepens each day for you.

It's hard not to kiss you, it's hard not to hold you in my arms and squeeze you, So that I can show you how much I adore you.

It's hard not to lie beside you and tell you baby I love you. It's hard not to walk beside you and hold your hands.

It's hard not to run and greet you. It's hard not to feel you breathing in my ear, as you take your nights rest with my arms wrapped tightly around you.

It's hard enough sitting alone thinking of you. It's hard enough dreaming about you; But when

I awake and I'm not with you, instead of going back to sleep I'll stay up and wait for you.

265. Do not expect perfection from your spouse for he/she is only human.

266. Create archives of memories–pictures, videos and ornaments as you journey together.

267. Forgive, forgive, you must learn how to forgive quickly.

268. Be watchful of the different mood swings, so you will know what to do and what to say. Know when to do nothing just give space, until that phase has past. (Just pray)

269. Determine what to say to your spouse.

270. Determine how to say things to your spouse.

271. Determine when to say it to your spouse.

272. Determine why you want to say it to your spouse.

273. Determine where you want to tell your spouse.

274. When both have agreed on a matter, do not break it, as it can cause tremors in the marriage.

275. Be honest with yourself and it will filter down into your marriage.

276. Think positive and positive vibes will permeate the marriage union.

277. As often as you can, re-enforce your love for each other – do it!

278. Try and make up for promises that were broken, it says something.

279. Visit your earthly counselor/s, but stay connected to your heavenly Counselor.

A Virtuous Woman

Wives respect and obey your husbands.

Wives in doing this, the husbands who do not know and obey the word of God will want to know about God. They will want to know who He is. Why? Because their wives, live good lives. You should not be fine on the outside only: you wear nice clothes, you wear the most expensive make-up, and gold is your preferred choice in jewelry.

Your hearts must also look good; it must be gentle, and quiet. For what is on the inside will radiate on the outside. God says that this is what he is looking for. Remember Sarah, she obeyed Abraham to the point of calling him lord.
Proverbs 31: 10-31

280. The price for a virtuous woman is far above rubies.

281. The heart of her husband trust in her.

282. She does her husband good and not evil. *"He who finds a wife finds what is good and receives favor from the Lord." (Proverbs. 18:22)*

283. She is willing with her hands. She hates to be idle.

284. She brings good food to her table.

285. She rise up to pray for her spouse while it is still night.

286. She gives to the poor and helps the needy. *"A wife of noble character is her husband's crown, but a disgraceful wife is like decay in his bones." (proverbs. 12:4)*

287. She is respected by others.

288. Her children and husband puts her in high esteem.

289. She cannot be compared to other women, for she is a cut above the rest.

290. And most importantly she is a woman who fears the Lord.

> *Entreat me not to leave you, or to turn back from following after you; for wherever you go, I will go; and wherever you lodge, I will lodge; your people shall be my people, and your god, my God.*

> *Where you die, I will die, and there will
> I be buried. The Lord do so to me and
> more also, if anything but death parts
> you and me." (Ruth 1:16-17)*

TESTIMONIAL 3

I met a young lady who shared in explicit details what happened to her and her husband.

She told me, they were married for ten years, both attended church within their community. After ten years, she just got complacent, reluctant, and carefree expecting her husband to love her continuously. She stopped looking sexy for him, due to the fact that she had put on a couple pounds. The union did not produce any children. She stopped combing her hair and having a bath before he reached home from work. She did not believe it would have caused problems, for heaven's sake the man was a deacon in the church. She thought she had arrived.

There began frequent arguments in the home, he started coming home later than usual, kissing had ended and he fasted from her company sexually.

A few months later, he asked her for a divorce; it never hit her during all that time of reluctance and withdrawal. That another woman wowed her husband out of her arms, her bed and his heart.

Wife, due to the fact that you and your husband are Christians, you think there's no need to do hard labor to keep him. But beware, for there are elements and she-devils out there, that by the time you could count 1, 2, 3 another has captivated his heart.

WIVES, TREAT YOUR HUSBAND'S RIGHT.

Likewise ye wives be in subjection to your own husband; that, if any obey not the word, they also may without the word be won by the conversation of the wives.

While they below your chaste conversation coupled with fear.

Whose adorning let it not be that outward adorning of plaiting the hair, and of wearing of gold, or of putting on of apparel;

But it be the hidden man of the heart, in that which is not corruptible, even the ornament of a meek and quiet spirit, which is in the sight of God of great price.

For after this manner in the old time the Holy women also, who trusted in God adorned themselves, being in subjection unto their own husbands. Even has Sara obeyed Abraham, calling him lord: whose daughters ye are, as long as ye do well, and are not afraid with any amazement? (1 Peter 3: 1-6)

291. A virtuous woman is firm and strong for her man.

292. A virtuous woman walks upright and fears God.

293. A virtuous woman stands down in her heart, even when flesh rises in the heat of an argument.

294. A virtuous woman breathes integrity, truth and prosperity.

295. A virtuous woman obeys her Husband.

296. A virtuous woman will uplift her husband with loyalty.

297. A virtuous woman will trust her husband in the midst of a dozen women.

298. A virtuous woman has a deep level of humility and inner strength.

299. A virtuous woman submits to her husband in her heart first.

300. A virtuous woman submits to unpleasant circumstances, for the sake of peace.

301. A virtuous woman does well and expects nothing in return.

302. A virtuous woman does not partake in anything that is consciously forbidden.

303. A virtuous woman stands on the rock who is Jesus Christ, stands with her husband and stand against the wrong.

304. An understanding wife welcomes openness and free speech within the marriage.

305. A submissive wife adorns herself appropriately.
"For after this manner in the old time the holy women also, who trusted in God, adorned themselves, being in subjection unto their own husbands." (1 Peter. 3:5)

306. A good Christian wife develops inner beauty.

307. Cooperate with your husband, agree to disagree.
"Submit to one another out of reverence for Christ." (Eph. 5:21)

308. Always win over your husband with the love you have for him.

309. Look good and sexy for your husband.

310. Do not be obsessive with today's fashion, but rather with passion towards Christ and your Spouse.

311. Live your Christianity right in your home and your husband and family can see Christ radiating on you.

312. Don't be too concern with everything else that you forget about you.

313. Fashion the home into a sweet haven of comfort and relaxation.

314. Saturate his surrounding with tranquility.

315. Have a good hygiene; this is especially important when you go out with your husband.

316. Have a sugary attitude and a sensitive spirit.

True Beauty Begins Within

317. Be a tower of support for your husband.

318. Fast and pray together for the same cause.

319. Break soul-ties and build new memories with your husband.

320. Communicate one hundred percent with each other.

321. Most importantly, respect, respect, and more respect towards your husband. *"Most important of all, continue to show deep love for each other, for love covers a multitude of sins." (1 Peter 4:8)*

322. Be of one mind with your husband.

323. Have a heart of compassion towards your husband.

324. Free your marriage from past emotional baggage.

325. Put your husband first and extended family second.

326. Love the fellowship with your husband.

327. Show diligence and compassion towards your lover.

328. Make yourself available to your husband at all times.

329. Cover the back of your husband with prayer, he is depending on you.

> *"¹⁰Finally, my brethren, be strong in the Lord, and in the power of his might. ¹¹Put on the whole armour of God, that ye may be able to stand against the wiles of the devil. ¹²For we wrestle not against flesh and blood, but against principalities, against powers, against the rulers of the darkness of this world, against spiritual wickedness in high places. ¹³Wherefore take unto you the whole armour of God, that ye may be able to withstand in the evil day, and having done all, to stand.*
>
> *¹⁴Stand therefore, having your loins girt about with truth, and having on the breastplate of righteousness; ¹⁵ And your feet shod with the preparation of the gospel of peace; ¹⁶Above all, taking the shield of faith, wherewith ye shall be able to quench all the fiery darts of the wicked. ¹⁷And take the helmet of salvation, and the sword of the Spirit, which is the word of God: ¹⁸Praying always with all prayer and supplication in the Spirit, and watching thereunto with all perseverance and supplication for all saints;" (Ephesians 6:10-18)*

330. Pray for a continuous edge around your husband.

331. Stand in the gap for your husband.

332. Be an ambassador for the marriage union.

333. Do not entertain lustful thoughts for another who is not your betrothed.

334. A virtuous woman will stand by her man through the various storms of life.

Husband
(Stand in your
Priestly Position)

Husbands, live with your wives the way you know is right. Respect her, because she is a woman. She is not as strong as a man. Also, respect her for God has given her to you. She is your blessing of life, for she will multiply you (your seeds) in due season. By doing this, you will not stop God from doing what you ask of him to do for you.

Care for her, when she is in trouble, Love her when you see her faults, be kind to her and stand proud of her when she succeed in life. Do not do wrong things to her because she does wrong things to you. Do not say wrong things to her because she says wrong things to you. Instead, ask God to bless her and by doing so God will in turn bless you.

Turn away from doing harm to her, try hard to find peace in the relationship, watch over her, listen and talk to her. Worship God together.

> *Husbands love your wives even as Christ loved the church and gave himself for it. So ought men to their wives as their own bodies. He that loveth his wife loveth himself. For no man ever yet hated his own flesh; but nourisheth and cherisheth it even as the Lord the church (Ephesians. 5:25, 28, 29)*

335. An honest husband has <u>one wife</u>. If there isn't honesty, trust can be destabilized and security destroyed.

336. A sincere husband is rooted firm in genuine love. He will not be afraid to sing her praises, in front of her and out of her presence. *"Behold, thou art fair; thou hast dove eyes. Behold, thou art fair, my beloved, yea, pleasant: also our bed is green." {Songs of Solomon 1:16}*

337. A loving husband acknowledge is partner and values her. Complements flow naturally and there lays no ulterior motives behind his love. *"Thy cheeks are comely with rows of jewels, thy neck with chains of gold." { Songs of Solomon 1:10}*

338. A caring husband is understanding, and does not show cruelty. *"You have captivated my heart, my sister, my bride; you have captivated my heart with one glance of your eyes, with one jewel of your necklace." (Songs of Solomon. 4:9)*

Husband (Stand in your Priestly Position)

339. A compassionate husband reciprocates and co-operates with his wife. His sincerity to be a good husband comes with good intentions.

340. A God fearing husband acknowledges biblical principles and Knows that God is his head. *"O my dove, that art in the cleft of the rock, in the secret places of the stairs, let me see the countenance, let me hear thy voice; for sweet is thy voice and thy countenance is comely." {Song of Solomon 2:14}*

341. A sympathetic husband is not a vindictive lover. He will understand that sex is not just for him to enjoy. But pleasing his wife is the way forward.

342. A loving husband does not verbally or physically abuse his wife. His love is gentle and never harsh; he avoids scratching his wife's face with his whiskers. *"His left hand is under my head, and his right hand doth embrace me." {Songs of Solomon 2:6}*

343. A godly husband recognize "she-devils" who lurks about to destroy his marital bliss.

344. A considerate husband will accept the things he cannot change about his wife and help to change that which they can together.

345. A good husband obtains honor from his wife and family and friends.

346. A loving husband is granted favor from God.

347. A caring husband will find a submissive wife. *"He brought me to the banqueting house, and his banner over me is love."* {Song of Solomon 2:5}

348. An obedient husband obeys God word in regards to himself and his wife

> *"Set me as a seal upon your heart, as a seal upon your arm, for love is strong as death, jealousy is fierce as the grave. Its flashes are flashes of fire, the very flame of the Lord. Many waters cannot quench love, neither can floods drown it. If a man offered for love all the wealth of his house, he would be utterly despised."* (Songs of Solomon 8:6-7)

¶LISTEN CAREFULLY

349. Husbands possess the inner strength to love your wife in spite of the emotional storms.

350. Husbands, you were not called to over-power or rule your wife with a long stick, but to love her.

351. Do not downgrade your wife in any way, shape or form.

352. Put more value on your wife not your

353. Possessions!

354. Be strong at heart; strong in thought; center your mind on the word of God.

355. Know when to admit that you're wrong.

356. Be a strong authoritative role model for your wife and family.

357. Bear your responsibilities with humility and joy.

358. Be prepared to handle financial problems mentally if it visits you.

359. Prevent seeking refuge in another woman's temple, if yours is leaking or have a fault – fix it and remain there!

360. Be man enough to be content with your woman, while you both work on the issues affecting the union.

361. Love God, love your wife and love others.

362. Allow your wife to see commitment glowing from your eyes.

363. Let the peace of God rule in your heart and abide in your home.

> *Likewise ye husbands, dwell with them according to knowledge, giving honor unto the wife, as unto the weaker vessel, and as being heirs together of the grace*

of life; that your prayer be not hindered.
(1 Peter 3: 7)

364. Withdraw into your own private world of romance with your wife.

365. Purge bitterness out of your heart, this can pollute your mind and your relationship.

366. Don't be a victim of stale love. Give love from the fountain of your heart and it will rush back to you in full measure.

367. Know your wife's favorite color.

368. Memorize her shoe size.

369. Remember her birthday.

370. Cook her favorite food.

371. Bear in your mind your first kiss together.

372. Be knowledgeable about your wedding day.

373. Know about your wife background and family ties.

374. Get acquainted with her height and weight.

375. Share with your soul-mate be familiar with her curves.

376. Most importantly, you are not afraid to look her straight in the eye and exalt her for a while.

377. Avoid self-pity and trust your partner in love crime.

378. Allow your rough times to be stepping stones to building a closer bond with your wife. *There are three things that amaze me-no, four things that I don't understand: How an eagle glides through the sky, how a snake slithers on a rock, how a ship navigates the ocean, how a man loves a woman." (Proverbs 30:18-19)*

Husbands Do Not...

379. Do not try to change her without her consent, it will cause conflict.

380. Do not be lazy at home.

381. Do not be aggressive to your wife.

382. *Then the Lord God said, 'it is not good that the man should be alone; I will make him a helper fit for him.' ....So the Lord caused a deep sleep to fall upon the man, and while he slept took one of his ribs and close up its place with flesh. And the rib that the lord God hath taken from man he made into a woman and brought her to the man." (Genesis 2:18-25)*

Commit to Happiness

Recipe 101 (Creole Poem)

Hug di woman, Bless di man.
Kiss di woman, Respec di man.
Chat good wid di woman,
Look good fi di man.
Love di woman, Cook fi di man.
Wok pan di woman, tan pan ni lang.
Mek sure she cum fus, den yu cum second
Stick wid di woman, Tan wi di man.
Pray pan di plan, Ovulate wid di man
But do, no lef di man weh gi you di plan.

God a di one weh gi you di woman.
So even wen tings a go wrong,
no tackle di woman and lick down di man.
Just check the same one weh did gi you di plan,
serious ting young man an woman.

Joycelyn Lawson

> *So God created man in his own image, in the image of God created he him, male and female created he them. And God bless them, and God said unto them, be fruitful and multiply, and replenish the earth, and subdue it, and have dominion over the fish of the sea, and over the fowl of the air, and over every living thing that moveth upon the earth. (Genesis 1: 27, 28)*

383. Expect good returns if you invest wisely in your marriage.

384. Expect true happiness, if the marriage is built on truth. 'I am the way the truth and the light, says the lord.'

COMMIT TO:

385. A life that is well- balanced.

386. A life that provides a high way to express the deepest desires of showing someone special and dear to your heart that you cannot do or live without them.

387. That life where your partner is the essence of your being, he /she make your world sweet.

388. A life of love and not infatuation.

389. A life of children breathing upon your youthfulness, bringing you joy and laughter.

390. A life of purity and beauty that goes deep beneath the skin.

391. A life that was intended for a couple who is equally yoked.

392. A life of its fullest freedom to express affection in open space and in the den of secrecy.

393. A life that does not have to justify why, how, who and where.

394. A life that demonstrates a close relationship with your spouse. And reap growth and development.

395. Expect a spiritual tsunami impact on your marriage if you become complacent, reluctant or lazy in its maintenance.

I'M COMMITTED (Poem)

I'm committed; I'm giving up my time for you.

Tell me what you desire of me to do.

I surrender to you my love,

I give in to your care,

> I submit to your passion, I withdraw into your defense,
>
> I crumble under your charm, and I melt in your arms of passion.
>
> I flourish when rapped in your love; I decline to fight against my protector. I prosper in your integrity, I increase in security. I enlarge in your sanctuary. (Joycelyn Lawson)

396. Commit to give your spouse a sense of belonging.

397. Commit to recognizing your spouse emotional needs.

398. Commit to endure the different stages of your marital cycle.

399. Commit to share serious passion.

400. Commit to make meaningful and fruitful conversation with your spouse.

401. Commit to solving your problems as soon as they develop.

402. Commit to protecting your spouse and family.

403. Commit to do things together as a couple.

404. Commit to apologizing when there happens to be a fall out with you and your soul-mate.

405. Commit to pleasing your spouse the best way, Gods way.

406. Commit to enjoying each other's company.

407. Commit to accepting your spouse appearance and appreciate the inner character.

408. Commit to mutual dependence on each other.

409. Commit to giving your all and not just apart.

410. Commit to demonstrate internal love by using external pleasures.

411. Commit to protecting the sanctity of your faithfulness to each other.

412. Commit to responsibility, not hard labor.

413. Commit to obedience, submission and respect.

414. Commit to positive influence and mentorship.

415. Commit to review your success and let it not be a hindrance to the success of your marriage.

416. Commit to stand accountable to labor.

417. Commit to practice the laws of God, to do your best and ensure a lasting friendship with your spouse.

418. Commit to allowing the Holy Spirit to be the senior partner in your partnership of marriage.

419. Commit to crying unto God for your spouse, He's ready to hear your prayer.

420. Commit to unending love and affection.

421. Commit to procreation and not abortion.

422. Commit to nurturing and not physical abuse to neither spouse and or children.

423. Commit to promotion and not stagnation in your life.

Express Yourself:

424. E - Eat the fruits of your labour.

425. X - xray my heart for you my love

426. P - Pick only from your tree.

427. R - Rest in your garden of love.

428. E - Eye contact, watch and learn.

429. S - Stay up and talk awhile.

430. S - Sleep, it was all good.

431. Y - You are my Eros love

432. O - Our love will never die.

433. U - Use me I'm yours for life.

434. R - Reap the harvest you have

435. sown.

436. S - See what you like?

437. E - Eat all you like.

438. L - Leave none behind.

439. F - For I am your delight.

Marriage is a Sacrifice

I was willing to surrender or sacrifice anything, to allow my marriage to flourish, because I know that committing to the union of marriage is a sacrifice. Nothing good comes easy in life. I have to sometimes fight against the odds.

So should you, if you love your spouse, you must be willing to lay down your very life in order to protect his or hers; Just as how God, Christ laid down his life for the ones He love, (The Church). The devil is here to steal, kill and destroy every good thing, and marriage is no exception. He loves to see discord, abuse, conflicts, disputes, frictions, disagreement, and division, separate and divorce.

The Love Pledge:

440. My love, I am sacrificing me for us to grow the union.

441. I'll sacrifice greener pastures, and water the grass I have at home.

442. I'll sacrifice my life, just to protect the love of my life.

443. I'll sacrifice my love to the world, just to please you my world.

444. I'll sacrifice the love for another, just to nourish the love I'll have forever.

445. I'll sacrifice conflicts, just to keep the romance ignited and alive.

446. I'll sacrifice sleep, just to await the return of my spouse out late at nights.

447. I'll sacrifice loneliness, just to lie in the arms of my soul mate at night.

448. I'll sacrifice solitude, just to pray with and for my spouse.

449. I'll sacrifice strife, just so my spouse and I will have sweet harmony.

450. I'll sacrifice silence, just to fellowship and dialogue with my spouse.

451. I'll sacrifice the company of idlers, So that quality time can be spent with my spouse.

Marriage is a Sacrifice

452. I'll sacrifice anger, just so my spouse and I can resolve our issues calmly.

453. I'll sacrifice long hours at work, just to spend quality time with my spouse.

454. I'll sacrifice the company of short term friends, just to be closer to my life long term friend.

455. I'll sacrifice the pleasures of this earth, just to enjoy the pleasures of my earthen vessel of love.

456. I'll sacrifice television, just to keep my focus and attention on my beloved spouse.

457. I'll sacrifice unnecessary work in order to dedicate more time to my spouse.

Ask and it shall be given; seek and ye shall find, knock and it shall be open unto you.

Get God's help to choose that right person for you, only he alone can see individuals for who they really are.

We can clearly see the external of a person; he/she looks good, looks humble, talks nicely, and or is well put together. But the heart can be totally opposite from what you see.

So it is important that you seek God for direction and make the right choices and then commit to making it work according to the standard Christ sets for the union of marriage.

458. Steal not water from another man's cistern, but drink running waters from your own stream.

459. Let the juice you swallow, be your own and not a stranger.

460. Intake the spring of sensual fuel from your wife's breasts.

❡Important to Note

A woman is like an iron, she'll take time to heat up but when she does, she will become very hot. On the other hand, men are likened to light bulbs, switched on, he's ready.

Some men sometimes neglect foreplay and third base petting because they desire a quick run.

Men, bring your wife to that point of no return; bring her to that point where she will be the one to lead you up Climax Mountain.

461. The immune system of love has to be nurtured and groomed in order to stay strong.

462. Your health is your wealth, and taking care of your spouse is treasured gift to the bearer of true love.

463. Assist your spouse to make the necessary steps to enriching the union of love.

464. The ideal responsibility of any couple in love is to bring stability to the relationship, by sticking together through times of adversities and complexities.

465. Allow your love to kiss you with the kisses of his lips.

466. Allow him to lie all night betwixt your breasts.

467. Don't be more focus on wealth, but more the health of your marriage.

1⇨2⇨3⇨ Red Light

Over the past decade, there has been reported a high increase in the divorce rate. Married Christian couples find themselves being separated or divorce after just five years of marriage. Individuals entered the marriage with a lot of baggage; this could be physical, emotional or spiritual. Not knowing how to deal with it, Termination of the union was the ultimate move.

The harsh reality is that the spouse within such union need to give a more earnest attention to the various hiccups that can shatter the union.

Let me illustrate my point. One of the games we played as children in Jamaica was called, "123 Red Light"; I would imagine that there is dissimilarity of this game in other part of the world. The basic principles of the game are as follows: One person (the caller), stands at one end of the playing field, while the other players stand at the other end. 'The Caller' turns his/her back to the others and calls out "123 red light!" As the call is made the players then run as fast as they can towards "the caller". At the end of the call, "the caller" will quickly turn around and face the players; the players must freeze in place.

If anyone fails to freeze, they are out or must return to the starting line. If "the caller" is fast enough to catch all the players or one at a time in their move, then "the caller" remains a head of the game.

However, if one of the players reaches and touches "the caller" before he/she finishes the call; "the caller" loses and no longer controls the game.

Consider each hiccup as a player trying to advance in an effort to get you out of the game. But remember, that you can stay in control and continue calling the "shots" if you are swift enough to indentify each of them in their moves and get them out of the game first.

So, go ahead, and stay in the game by indentifying some of these shortcomings.

Some are stated below:-

468. Soul-ties from past relationships have not been severed.

469. The relationship was built on a foundation of lies.

470. Relationship was infected by a spirit of deception.

471. Infatuation was the core/foundation of the relationship.

472. Sex took the heart of the relationship, not God and his love.

473. Mistrust and unfaithfulness were uninvited guests that enter the relationship and cause problems.

474. Sexual infidelity is the number one cause for marriages to fail

475. Both parties were unequally yoked. Couples are not equal which causes decision making to become difficult.

476. Constant arguing in the marriage. Couples were unable to communicate honestly with each other.

477. Lack of intimacy. One or both partners are not sexually satisfied, so he/she ends up having sex with someone who is not their spouse.

478. Monologue now exist in the marriage when dialogue went into retirement. The relationship is left grasping for breathe to stay alive.

479. Togetherness refused to fight for love so hatred and bitterness move into the marriage.

480. Tiredness, monologue, sleeplessness, headaches, irritability causes the marriage to contract upset stomach.

481. There lies difficulty in making conscious decisions.

482. Spouse gained excessive weight. Hence, the marriage dies due to obesity. *I don't like how you look any more, I need someone prettier or more handsome. You are not the body type I married to.*

483. Worry introduces crying/stress which eventually leads to Heart attack or the untimely breaking down of the union.

484. Adultery is a poison that sends the relationship into a marital coma.

485. The symptoms of frustration was evident, the real issues were neglected.

486. By the time the causes are identified, the marriage is on the rocks and divorce papers are already signed.

> *For the commandment is a lamp; and the law is light; and reproof of instructions are the way of life, to keep thee from the evil women, from the flattery of the tongue of a strange woman.*
> *Lust not after her beauty in thine heart; neither let her take thee with her eye lids. For by means of a whorish woman a man is brought to a piece of bread; and the adulteress will hunt for the precious life. (Proverbs 6: 23-26)*

487. You allowed family to have an input in decision making.

488. Spouse feels neglected and not appreciated in the relationship.

489. The spouse under went verbal and physical abuse.

490. You allowed work to take center stage in your life.

491. You simply fell out of grace with your God and spouse.

492. When anxiety kicks him, you fail to communicate, you ignore your spouse out of your life.

493. You'll preferably share your heart with a colleague and not the one closest to you, your neck, your vertebra, your spouse.

494. Instead of having two breasts to feed on, there are four.

495. Instead of having one sex partner, there are two sometimes more.

496. The relationship becomes a pressured, and not gratifying.

497. The sexual tension has erupted as like a troubled volcano.

498. The couple hesitates to ask for help.

499. There was no room for forgiveness.

500. Self-centeredness plays the main role in the marital relationship.

501. The couple did not value God's intervention in the relationship.

502. The relationship lacked commitment.

503. There lacked respect for each other in the marriage.

504. There lacked understanding in the marriage

505. There lacked consideration in the marriage.

506. There lacked co-operation among each other.

507. There lacked Faithfulness in the marriage.

508. There lacked trustworthiness in the marriage.

509. There lacked consistency in the marriage.

510. There lacked obedience in the marriage.

511. There lacked fulfillment in the marriage.

512. There lacked submission in the marriage.

Consider this scenario: "A man was passing a farmers field, he looked over and saw a red apple. He was hungry, what should he do?

- ♥ Should he climb the farmer's fence, and touch, squeeze or even pick the apple that is not his?

- ♥ Should he knock at the farmer's gate, and ask if he could have the apple he saw on the tree in his field?

The proper, most descent thing to do is to ask, then with his authorization you can eat and be filled. So (b.) is good to go.

It is my personal conviction from the "Word of God" that a born again Christian should not have sex before the covenant of marriage is made. 1 Corinthians 15:20;

1 Corinthians 7: 2, and Colossians 3:5; The bible promotes total abstinence before marriage. The only sexual relationship that God agrees to is "husbands and Wives"

In my Jamaican Culture it is said, "Mi nah buy puss in a bag". Or "mi ave fi taste di cookie, before mi buy it". Meaning, we have to have sex before we get married. The woman may not have a vaginal opening. And the man may be impotent meaning *(they cannot have an erection, or even more, stay up long even to finish love making.)*

My response to this is, we are no "puss" nor are we cookies, but rather, sons and daughters of the Most High God, who is our Father. Neither are we confined to a bag, but we have been translated into His Kingdom of light. God hath delivered us from the power of darkness, and hath translated us into the kingdom of his dear son. (Colossians. 1:13) We are a Royal Priesthood called to be holy in this present world. *"But ye are a chosen generation, a royal priesthood, an holy nation, a peculiar people; that ye should shew froth the praises of him who hath called you out of darkness into his marvelous light." (1 Peter 2:9)*

Furthermore, if the sex before marriage is to prove your love, then it only disapproves your love and respect for the person, and God. A word to the wise, you cannot finish sex, but having unprotected sex with multiple partners can bring you to an early grave.

Let us be realistic, there is no way you can have magnet and steel in the same corner and they don't touch or connect. *"Can a man take fire in his bosom and his clothes not be burned? Can one go upon hot coals, and his feet not be burned?" (Proverbs. 6:27, 28)*

513. There lacked discipline among married couples.

514. There lacked restraint in vulgarity in the relationship toward a spouse.

515. There was more chaos, than there was peace.

516. Pretence flowed like a river right into the sea of divorce.

517. There were varying masks worn in the relationship.

518. There were changeable moods that over whelmed the relationship.

519. Love was unstable, thus relationship crumbled under the pressure.

520. There were too many excuses and little or no reasoning.

521. Couple's behavior towards each other was undermining.

522. Depression choked the marriage to divorce.

523. Rejection turned forgiveness away.

524. Rebellion coveted love and override obedience.

Testimonial 4

Six years into her marriage, Deb's husband recovered from an accident that nearly killed him. Then he decided it was time to live his life to the fullest. With no regard for his family, he quit his job, no longer provided for Deb and her children and stayed out nightly 'til 3:00 a.m. with no explanation of his whereabouts. Not knowing where to turn, Deb escaped the turmoil by divorcing him.

Deb then married a second husband who seemed compassionate about all she had been through in her first marriage. But five years into her second marriage, her husband became abusive toward her children and ended up having a three-year affair with another woman. When Deb discovered the affair, she left the marriage and swore off men, wanting nothing to do with another marriage or relationship.

It was then that God began to show Deb the kind of husband *He* could be toward her: her Provider, her Protector, her Counselor, and her Friend. *"For your Maker is your husband—the LORD Almighty is his name…. The LORD will call you back as if you were a wife deserted and distressed in spirit—a wife who married young, only to be rejected," says your God."(Isaiah 54:10)*

As Deb began to grow in her relationship with God, she began to see the many ways He could husband her and she realized she didn't need to keep looking for a man to marry. She had all she needed in God.

"I told God I didn't need a man as long as I had Him!" Deb told me, as she recalled her story. That was when God unexpectedly brought Dave into Deb's life. Dave was committed to God and was able to show Deb what a godly marriage looked like. Together, Dave and Deb now serve God through various ministries at their church. But Deb is convinced she had to first look to God to be her husband, before she could recognize a godly man. (extract-Cindi McMenamin Author)

123 Red Light

525. Work took precedence over the companionship of the one you love.

526. Revolutionary change from love to hate

527. Revolutionary change from God to sin.

528. Revolutionary change from your spouse's bed, to a cheap motel room.

529. Radical move from the opposite sex to the same sex.

530. Each new resentment piles into a mountain before you could see it

531. Emotionally you're done, spiritually you are dead, mentally you are drain, and hence, physically the marriage comes to an end.

532. A spouse insists that the problem is the other partner and not the influence of the devil.

533. Instead of fighting for, you fight against. Instead of praying for, you pray against with hurtful words.

534. Lack of love, friendship, relationship.

535. The marriage union became a prison, because the one you love no longer loves you back.

536. Infatuation mistaken for love, lasted only for a while. And the pain to birth love in the marriage sends the heart in an emotional coma. With no vital

movements, the till death do us part machine has been turned off.

537. The heart overheated, for the marriage ran out of love. The marriage is no longer workable for God its creator was evicted years ago.

> *Marriage is to be honored by all, and husbands and wives must be faithful to each other. God will judge those who are immoral and those who commit adultery. (Hebrew 13:4)*

Conclusion

God in His infallible word gives clear instructions on how to best experience romance in all its fullness, and how to love our spouse in words and actions. Sex in marriage is undoubtedly one the best gifts given by God to man. We are commanded to procreate, respect, cherish, love, submit and obey and the list goes on.

Whether you are married, engaged to be married or thinking about marriage, you must first love yourself, before trying to love someone else. It is profoundly clear, that if you love yourself, you will not seek to harm yourself; You will not say unkind words to yourself.

God views marriage as a sacred relationship. Therefore, as Christians, we need to succeed in cherishing that which God as entrusted to us. From the beginning, God hath intended the union of marriage to be a blessed one. sexual fulfillment, joy of companionship and the art of procreation.

You see, His glorious plan was not completed until he made man and woman.

There are hurdles that as couples
we must cross over, in spite of the short
comings of our first couple, Adam and Eve,
God's mind has not changed about marriage.
Hence, he made a way out. He asked of us to
read His word and live His word and
everything else he will take care of.

Husbands, you are the head, lead your family
in the way of the Lord, listen for His still small voice
and not another. Be the stronger
vessel which you are and protect, love and
respect your wife, just as how Christ the
husband, loves the church his bride and died
for her. Put no one before her, the bible says,
leave and cleave. If there is a fault in her,
discuss it, pray about it and God will help you through it.

Wife, one of the things that a man values the most is a submissive wife; not one who is over bearing and stubborn. You sometimes being a go getter will unconsciously out rank him in being the provider and protector, this in its full essence makes him weak and sometimes pushes him into his manly cave. There, he locks himself away from you his wife. Hence, be <u>his</u> neck and not <u>the</u> head.

MARRIAGE IS AN HONORABLE THING, COMMIT TO HONOR IT.

www.ingramcontent.com/pod-product-compliance
Ingram Content Group UK Ltd.
Pitfield, Milton Keynes, MK11 3LW, UK
UKHW041944230426
12048UKWH00008B/130